HOW TO DRAW
A SIMPLE STEP BY STEP GUIDE FOR KIDS

Copyright 2015

How to use the book

. . .

Copy the simple steps
on the blank page to
learn how to draw
the animal or object!

This Book Belongs to

_____

Draw the Vampire Bat

Draw the Cute Dolphin

Draw the Happy Horse

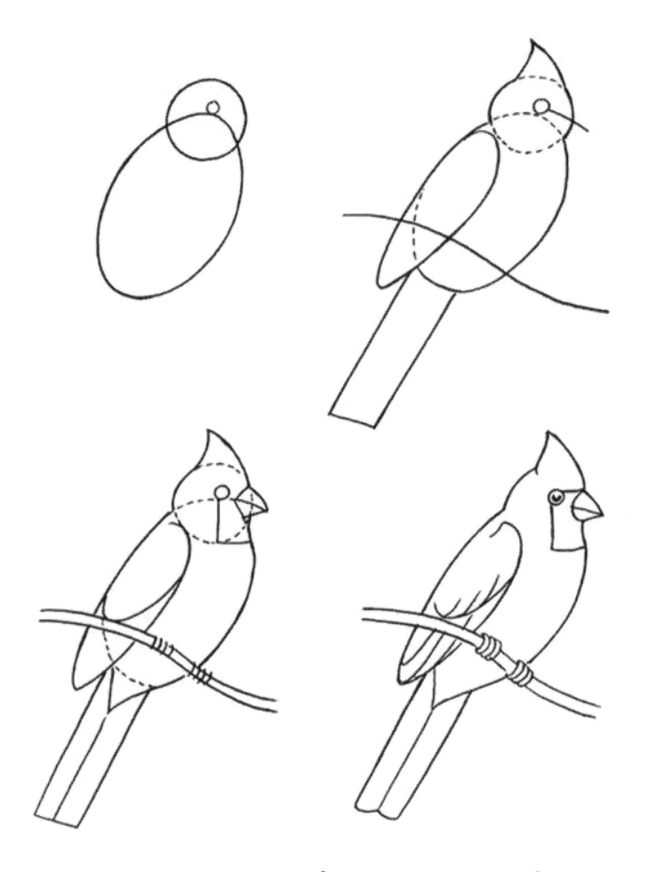

Draw the Chirpy Cardinal

Draw the Little Bird

Draw the Cute Bird

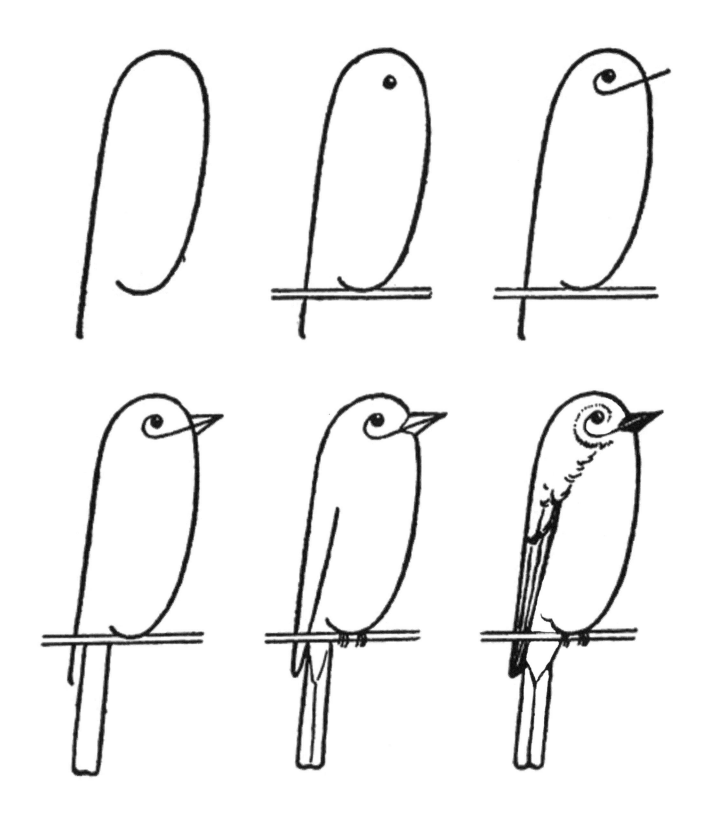

Draw the Bird on its Perch

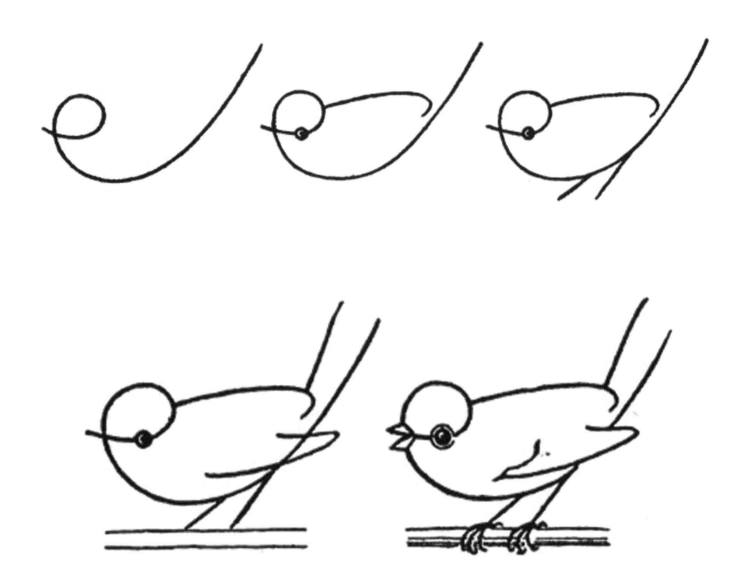

Draw the Songbird

Draw the Wise Owl

Draw the Kitty Cat

Draw the Cute Doggy

Draw the Mr. Frog

Draw the Taxi Cab

Draw the Cute Mouse

Draw the Happy Elephant

Draw the Halloween Bat

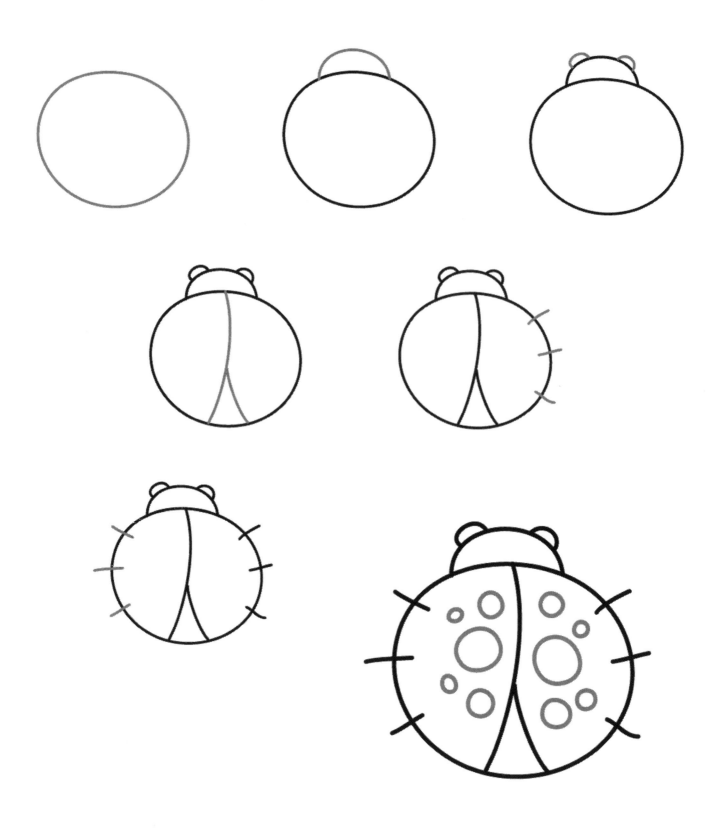

Draw the Ladybug

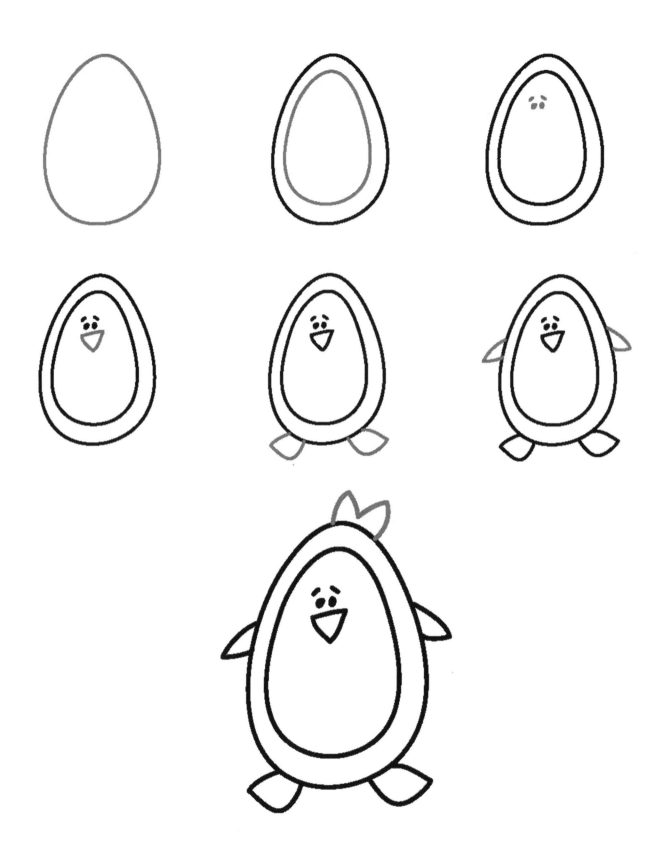

Draw the Pretty Penguin

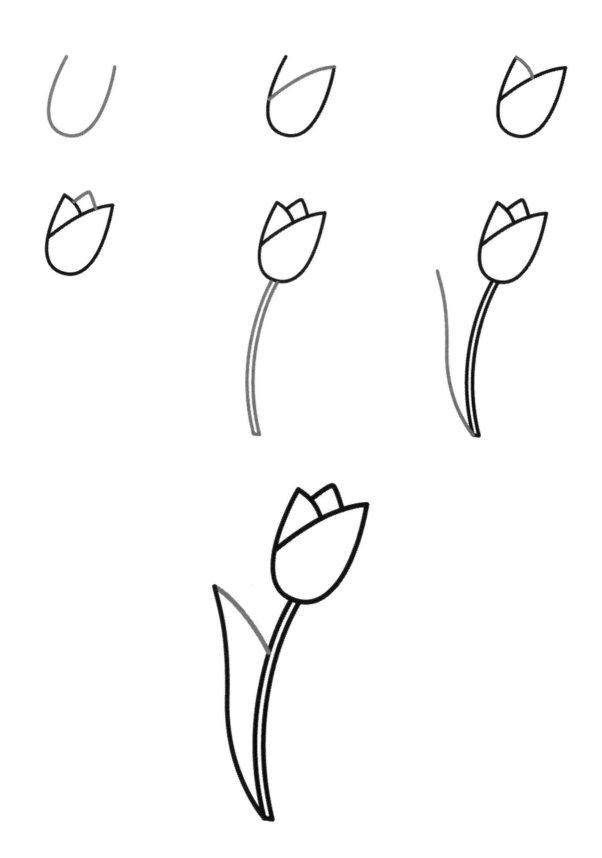

Draw the Pretty Tulips

Draw the Elephant

Awesome!
You are now a
Drawing Pro

Use the next few
pages to test your
Drawing Skills